Getting and Finding Advertising, Marketing, Promotions, Public Relations, and Sales Managers Jobs

—

The Ultimate Guide for Job Seekers and Recruiters

ADVERTISING, MARKETING, PROMOTIONS, PUBLIC RELATIONS, AND SALES MANAGER JOBS

Copyright

ADVERTISING, MARKETING, PROMOTIONS, PUBLIC RELATIONS, AND SALES MANAGER JOBS

TABLE OF CONTENTS

ADVERTISING, MARKETING, PROMOTIONS, PUBLIC RELATIONS, AND SALES MANAGER JOBS

INTRODUCTION

For the first time, a book exists that compiles all the information candidates need to apply for their first Advertising, Marketing, Promotions, Public Relations, and Sales Managers job, or to apply for a better job.

What you'll find especially helpful are the worksheets. It is so much easier to write about a work experience using these outlines. It ensures that the narrative will follow a logical structure and reminds you not to leave out the most important points. With this book, you'll be able to revise your application into a much stronger document, be much better prepared and a step ahead for the next opportunity.

The book comes filled with useful cheat sheets. It helps you get your career organized in a tidy, presentable fashion. It also will inspire you to produce some attention-grabbing cover letters that convey your skills persuasively and attractively in your application packets.

After studying it, too, you'll be prepared for interviews, or you will be after you conducted the practice sessions where someone sits and asks you potential questions. It makes you think on your feet!

This book makes a world of difference in helping you stay away from vague and long-winded answers and you will be finally able to connect with prospective employers, including the one that will actually hire you.

This book successfully challenges conventional job search wisdom and doesn't load you with useful but obvious suggestions ("don't forget to wear a nice suit to your interview," for example). Instead, it deliberately challenges conventional job search wisdom, and in so doing, offers radical but inspired suggestions for success.

Think that "companies approach hiring with common sense, logic, and good business acumen and consistency?" Think that "the most qualified candidate gets the job?" Think again! Time and again it is proven that finding a job is a highly subjective business filled with innumerable variables. The triumphant jobseeker is the one who not only recognizes these inconsistencies and but also uses them to his advantage. Not sure how to do this? Don't worry-How to Land a Top-Paying Advertising, Marketing, Promotions, Public Relations, and Sales Managers Job guides the way.

Highly recommended to any harried Advertising, Marketing, Promotions, Public Relations, and Sales Managers jobseeker, whether you want to work for the government or a company. You'll plan on using it again in your efforts to move up in the world for an even better position down the road.

ADVERTISING, MARKETING, PROMOTIONS, PUBLIC RELATIONS, AND SALES MANAGER JOBS

This book offers excellent, insightful advice for everyone from entry-level to senior professionals. None of the other such career guides compare with this one. It stands out because it: 1) explains how the people doing the hiring think, so that you can win them over on paper and then in your interview; 2) has an engaging, reader-friendly style; 3) explains every step of the job-hunting process - from little-known ways for finding openings to getting ahead on the job.

This book covers everything. Whether you are trying to get your first Advertising, Marketing, Promotions, Public Relations, and Sales Managers job or move up in the system, get this book.

ADVERTISING, MARKETING, PROMOTIONS, PUBLIC RELATIONS, AND SALES MANAGER JOBS

ADVERTISING, MARKETING, PROMOTIONS, PUBLIC RELATIONS, AND SALES MANAGERS – THE LOWDOWN

- Nature of the Work
- Training, Other Qualifications, and Advancement
- Employment
- Job Outlook
- Projections Data
- Earnings
- OES Data
- Related Occupations
- Sources of Additional Information

Significant Points

- Keen competition is expected for these highly coveted jobs.
- College graduates with related experience, a high level of creativity, strong communication skills, and computer skills should have the best job opportunities.
- High earnings, substantial travel, and long hours, including evenings and weekends, are common.
- Because of the importance and high visibility of their jobs, these managers often are prime candidates for advancement to the highest ranks.

ADVERTISING, MARKETING, PROMOTIONS, PUBLIC RELATIONS, AND SALES MANAGER JOBS

Nature of the Work

Advertising, marketing, promotions, public relations, and sales managers coordinate their companies' market research, marketing strategy, sales, advertising, promotion, pricing, product development, and public relations activities. In small firms, the owner or chief executive officer might assume all advertising, promotions, marketing, sales, and public relations responsibilities. In large firms, which may offer numerous products and services nationally or even worldwide, an executive vice president directs overall advertising, marketing, promotions, sales, and public relations policies.

Advertising managers. Advertising managers oversee advertising and promotion staffs, which usually are small, except in the largest firms. In a small firm, managers may serve as liaisons between the firm and the advertising or promotion agency to which many advertising or promotional functions are contracted out. In larger firms, advertising managers oversee in-house account, creative, and media services departments. The *account executive* manages the account services department, assesses the need for advertising and, in advertising agencies, maintains the accounts of clients. The creative services department develops the subject matter and presentation of advertising. The *creative director* oversees the copy chief, art director, and associated staff. The *media director* oversees planning groups that select the communication media—for example, radio, television, newspapers, magazines, the Internet, or outdoor signs—to disseminate the advertising.

Marketing managers. Marketing managers develop the firm's marketing strategy in detail. With the help of subordinates, including *product development managers* and *market research managers,* they estimate the demand for products and services offered by the firm and its competitors. In addition, they identify potential markets—for example, business firms, wholesalers, retailers, government, or the general public. Marketing managers develop pricing strategy to help firms maximize profits and market share while ensuring that the firm's customers are satisfied. In collaboration with sales, product development, and other managers, they monitor trends that indicate the need for new products and services, and they oversee product development. Marketing managers work with advertising and promotion managers to promote the firm's products and services and to attract potential users.

Promotions managers. Promotions managers supervise staffs of promotions specialists. These managers direct promotions programs that combine advertising with purchase incentives to increase sales. In an effort to establish closer contact with purchasers—dealers, distributors, or consumers—promotions programs may use direct mail, telemarketing, television or radio advertising, catalogs, exhibits, inserts in newspapers, Internet advertisements or Web sites, in-store displays or product endorsements, and special events. Purchasing incentives may include discounts, samples, gifts, rebates, coupons, sweepstakes, and contests.

Public relations managers. Public relations managers supervise public relations specialists. (See the *Handbook* statement on public relations specialists.) These managers direct publicity programs to a targeted audience. They often specialize in a specific area, such as crisis management, or in a specific industry, such as health care. They use every available communication medium to maintain the support of the specific group upon whom their organization's success depends, such as consumers, stockholders, or the general public. For example, public relations managers may clarify or justify the firm's point of view on health or environmental issues to community or special-interest groups.

Public relations managers also evaluate advertising and promotions programs for compatibility with public relations efforts and serve as the eyes and ears of top management. They observe social, economic, and political trends that might ultimately affect the firm, and they make recommendations to enhance the firm's image on the basis of those trends.

Public relations managers may confer with labor relations managers to produce internal company communications—such as newsletters about employee-management relations—and with financial managers to produce company reports. They assist company executives in drafting speeches, arranging interviews, and maintaining other forms of public contact; oversee company archives; and respond to requests for information. In addition, some of these managers handle special events, such as the sponsorship of races, parties introducing new products, or other activities that the firm supports in order to gain public attention through the press without advertising directly.

Sales managers. Sales managers direct the firm's sales program. They assign sales territories, set goals, and establish training programs for the sales representatives. (See the *Handbook* statement on sales representatives, wholesale and manufacturing). Sales managers advise the sales representatives on ways to improve their sales performance. In large, multi-product firms, they oversee regional and local sales managers and their staffs. Sales managers maintain contact with dealers and distributors. They analyze sales statistics gathered by their staffs to determine sales potential and inventory requirements and to monitor customers' preferences. Such information is vital in the development of products and the maximization of profits.

Work environment. Advertising, marketing, promotions, public relations, and sales managers work in offices close to those of top managers. Working under pressure is unavoidable when schedules change and problems arise, but deadlines and goals must still be met.

Substantial travel may be involved. For example, attendance at meetings sponsored by associations or industries often is mandatory. Sales managers travel to national, regional, and local offices and to the offices of various dealers and distributors. Advertising and promotions managers may travel to meet with clients or representatives of communications media. At times, public relations managers travel to meet with special-interest groups or government officials. Job transfers between headquarters and regional offices are common, particularly among sales managers.

Long hours, including evenings and weekends are common. In last year, about two-thirds of advertising, marketing, and public relations managers worked more than 40 hours a week.

Training, Other Qualifications, and Advancement

A wide range of educational backgrounds is suitable for entry into advertising, marketing, promotions, public relations, and sales managerial jobs, but many employers prefer those with experience in related occupations.

Education and training. For marketing, sales, and promotions management positions, some employers prefer a bachelor's or master's degree in business administration with an emphasis on marketing. Courses in business law, management, economics, accounting, finance, mathematics, and statistics are advantageous. Additionally, the completion of an internship while the candidate is in school is highly recommended. In highly technical industries, such as computer and electronics manufacturing, a bachelor's degree in engineering or science, combined with a master's degree in business administration, is preferred.

For advertising management positions, some employers prefer a bachelor's degree in advertising or journalism. A course of study should include, for example, marketing, consumer behavior, market research, sales, communication methods and technology, and visual arts, and art history and photography.

ADVERTISING, MARKETING, PROMOTIONS, PUBLIC RELATIONS, AND SALES MANAGER JOBS

For public relations management positions, some employers prefer a bachelor's or master's degree in public relations or journalism. The applicant's curriculum should include courses in advertising, business administration, public affairs, public speaking, political science, and creative and technical writing.

Most advertising, marketing, promotions, public relations, and sales management positions are filled by promoting experienced staff or related professional personnel. For example, many managers are former sales representatives, purchasing agents, buyers, or product, advertising, promotions, or public relations specialists. In small firms, where the number of positions is limited, advancement to a management position usually comes slowly. In large firms, promotion may occur more quickly.

Other qualifications. Familiarity with word-processing and database applications is important for most positions. Computer skills are vital because marketing, product promotion, and advertising on the Internet are increasingly common. Also, the ability to communicate in a foreign language may open up employment opportunities in many rapidly growing areas around the country, especially cities with large Spanish-speaking populations.

ADVERTISING, MARKETING, PROMOTIONS, PUBLIC RELATIONS, AND SALES MANAGER JOBS

Persons interested in becoming advertising, marketing, promotions, public relations, and sales managers should be mature, creative, highly motivated, resistant to stress, flexible, and decisive. The ability to communicate persuasively, both orally and in writing, with other managers, staff, and the public is vital. These managers also need tact, good judgment, and exceptional ability to establish and maintain effective personal relationships with supervisory and professional staff members and client firms.

Certification and advancement. Some associations offer certification programs for these managers. Certification—an indication of competence and achievement—is particularly important in a competitive job market. While relatively few advertising, marketing, promotions, public relations, and sales managers currently are certified, the number of managers who seek certification is expected to grow. Today, there are numerous management certification programs based on education and job performance. In addition, The Public Relations Society of America offers a certification program for public relations practitioners based on years of experience and performance on an examination.

Although experience, ability, and leadership are emphasized for promotion, advancement can be accelerated by participation in management training programs conducted by larger firms. Many firms also provide their employees with continuing education opportunities—either in-house or at local colleges and universities—and encourage employee participation in seminars and conferences, often held by professional societies. In collaboration with colleges and universities, numerous marketing and related associations sponsor national or local management training programs. Course subjects include brand and product management, international marketing, sales management evaluation, telemarketing and direct sales, interactive marketing, promotion, marketing communication, market research, organizational communication, and data-processing systems procedures and management. Many firms pay all or part of the cost for employees who successfully complete courses.

Because of the importance and high visibility of their jobs, advertising, marketing, promotions, public relations, and sales managers often are prime candidates for advancement to the highest ranks. Well-trained, experienced, and successful managers may be promoted to higher positions in their own or another firm; some become top executives. Managers with extensive experience and sufficient capital may open their own businesses.

ADVERTISING, MARKETING, PROMOTIONS, PUBLIC RELATIONS, AND SALES MANAGER JOBS

Employment

Advertising, marketing, promotions, public relations, and sales managers held about 583,000 jobs in last year. The following tabulation shows the distribution of jobs by occupational specialty:

Sales managers	318,000
Marketing managers	167,000
Public relations managers	50,000
Advertising and promotions managers	47,000

These managers were found in virtually every industry. Sales managers held more than half of the jobs; most were employed in wholesale trade, retail trade, manufacturing, and finance and insurance industries. Marketing managers held more than a fourth of the jobs; the professional, scientific, and technical services, and the finance and insurance industries employed almost one-third of marketing managers.

About one-fourth of advertising and promotions managers worked in the professional, scientific, and technical services industries and the wholesale trade. Most public relations managers were employed in service-

providing industries, such as professional,
scientific, and technical services; educational
services, public and private; finance and
insurance; and health care and social
assistance.

Job Outlook

Average job growth is projected, but keen competition is expected for these highly coveted jobs.

Employment change. Employment of advertising, marketing, promotions, public relations, and sales managers is expected to increase by 12 percent through 2016—about as fast as the average for all occupations. Job growth will be spurred by intense domestic and global competition in products and services offered to consumers and increasing activity in television, radio, and outdoor advertising. Projected employment growth varies by industry. For example, employment is projected to grow much faster than average in scientific, professional, and related services—such as computer systems design and related services, and advertising and related services—as businesses increasingly hire contractors for these services instead of additional full-time staff. By contrast, a decline in employment is expected in many manufacturing industries.

Job prospects. Advertising, marketing, promotions, public relations, and sales manager jobs are highly coveted and will be sought by other managers or highly experienced professionals, resulting in keen competition. College graduates with related experience, a high level of creativity, and strong communication skills should have the

best job opportunities. In particular, employers
will seek those who have the computer skills to
conduct advertising, marketing, promotions,
public relations, and sales activities on the
Internet.

ADVERTISING, MARKETING, PROMOTIONS, PUBLIC RELATIONS, AND SALES MANAGER JOBS

Projection Data

Occupational title	SOC Code	Employment, last year	Projected employment, 2016	Change, last year-16	
				Number	Percent
Advertising, marketing, promotions, public relations, and sales managers	11-2000	583,000	651,000	68,000	12
Advertising and promotions managers	11-2011	47,000	50,000	3,000	6
Marketing and sales managers	11-2020	486,000	542,000	57,000	12
Marketing managers	11-2021	167,000	192,000	24,000	14
Sales managers	11-2022	318,000	351,000	33,000	10
Public relations managers	11-2031	50,000	58,000	8,400	17

NOTE: Data in this table are rounded.

ADVERTISING, MARKETING, PROMOTIONS, PUBLIC RELATIONS, AND SALES MANAGER JOBS

Earnings

Median annual earnings in May last year were $73,060 for advertising and promotions managers, $98,720 for marketing managers, $91,560 for sales managers, and $82,180 for public relations managers.

Median annual earnings of wage and salary advertising and promotions managers in May last year in the advertising and related services industry were $97,540.

Median annual earnings in the industries employing the largest numbers of marketing managers were:

Computer systems design and related services	$119,540
Management of companies and enterprises	103,070
Management, scientific, and technical consulting services	100,200
Architectural, engineering, and related services	92,480
Depository credit intermediation	91,420

ADVERTISING, MARKETING, PROMOTIONS, PUBLIC RELATIONS, AND SALES MANAGER JOBS

Median annual earnings in the industries employing the largest numbers of sales managers were:

Professional and commercial equipment and supplies merchant wholesalers	$112,810
Wholesale electronic markets and agents and brokers	107,420
Automobile dealers	101,110
Management of companies and enterprises	98,240
Machinery, equipment, and supplies merchant wholesalers	93,450

Salary levels vary substantially, depending upon the level of managerial responsibility, length of service, education, size of firm, location, and industry. For example, manufacturing firms usually pay these managers higher salaries than nonmanufacturing firms. For sales managers, the size of their sales territory is another important determinant of salary. Many managers earn bonuses equal to 10 percent or more of their salaries.

ADVERTISING, MARKETING, PROMOTIONS, PUBLIC RELATIONS, AND SALES MANAGER JOBS

According to a survey by the National Association of Colleges and Employers, starting salaries for marketing majors graduating in 2007 averaged $40,161 and those for advertising majors averaged $33,831.

Related Occupations

Advertising, marketing, promotions, public relations, and sales managers direct the sale of products and services offered by their firms and the communication of information about their firms' activities. Other workers involved with advertising, marketing, promotions, public relations, and sales include actors, producers, and directors; advertising sales agents; artists and related workers; demonstrators, product promoters, and models; market and survey researchers; public relations specialists; sales representatives, wholesale and manufacturing; and writers and editors.

Sources of Additional Information

For information about careers in advertising management, contact:

- American Association of Advertising Agencies, 405 Lexington Ave., New York, NY 10174-1801. Internet: http://www.aaaa.org

Information about careers and professional certification in public relations management is available from:

- Public Relations Society of America, 33 Maiden Lane, New York, NY 10038-5150. Internet: http://www.prsa.org

FINDING AND APPLYING FOR ADVERTISING, MARKETING, PROMOTIONS, PUBLIC RELATIONS, AND SALES MANAGERS JOBS AND EVALUATING OFFERS

Finding—and getting—a job you want can be a challenging process, but knowing more about job search methods and application techniques can increase your chances of success. And knowing how to judge the job offers you receive makes it more likely that you will end up with the best possible job.

- Where to learn About Job Openings
- Job Search Methods
- Applying for a Job
- Job Interview Tips
- Evaluating a Job Offer

Where to Learn About Job Openings

- Personal contacts
- School career planning and placement offices
- Employers
- Classified ads:
    i. National and local newspapers
    ii. Professional journals
    iii. Trade magazines
- Internet resources
- Professional associations
- Labor unions
- State employment service offices
- Federal Government
- Community agencies
- Private employment agencies and career consultants
- Internships

Job Search Methods

Finding a job can take months of time and effort. But you can speed the process by using many methods to find job openings. Data from the Bureau of Labor Statistics suggest that people who use many job search methods find jobs faster than people who use only one or two.

Personal contacts. Many jobs are never advertised. People get them by talking to friends, family, neighbors, acquaintances, teachers, former coworkers, and others who know of an opening. Be sure to tell people that you are looking for a job because the people you know may be some of the most effective resources for your search. To develop new contacts, join student, community, or professional organizations.

School career planning and placement offices. High school and college placement offices help their students and alumni find jobs. Some invite recruiters to use their facilities for interviews or career fairs. They also may have lists of open jobs. Most also offer career counseling, career testing, and job search advice. Some have career resource libraries; host workshops on job search strategy, resume writing, letter writing, and effective interviewing; critique drafts of resumes;

conduct mock interviews; and sponsor job fairs.

Employers. Directly contacting employers is one of the most successful means of job hunting. Through library and Internet research, develop a list of potential employers in your desired career field. Then call these employers and check their Web sites for job openings. Web sites and business directories can tell you how to apply for a position or whom to contact. Even if no open positions are posted, do not hesitate to contact the employer: You never know when a job might become available. Consider asking for an informational interview with people working in the career you want to learn more. Ask them how they got started, what they like and dislike about the work, what type of qualifications are necessary for the job, and what type of personality succeeds in that position. In addition to giving you career information, they may be able to put you in contact with other people who might hire you, and they can keep you in mind if a position opens up.

Classified ads. The "Help Wanted" ads in newspapers and the Internet list numerous jobs, and many people find work by responding to these ads. But when using classified ads, keep the following in mind:

- Follow all leads to find a job; do not rely solely on the classifieds.

- Answer ads promptly, because openings may be filled quickly, even before the ad stops appearing in the paper.
- Read the ads every day, particularly the Sunday edition, which usually includes the most listings.
- Keep a record of all ads to which you have responded, including the specific skills, educational background, and personal qualifications required for the position.

Internet resources. The Internet includes many job hunting Web sites with job listings. Some job boards provide National listings of all kinds; others are local. Some relate to a specific type of work; others are general. To find good prospects, begin with an Internet search using keywords related to the job you want. Also look for the sites of related professional associations.

Also consider checking Internet forums, also called message boards. These are online discussion groups where anyone may post and read messages. Use forums specific to your profession or to career-related topics to post questions or messages and to read about the job searches or career experiences of other people.

In online job databases, remember that job listings may be posted by field or discipline, so begin your search using keywords. Many Web sites allow job seekers to post their resumes online for free.

Professional associations. Many professions have associations that offer employment information, including career planning, educational programs, job listings, and job placement. To use these services, associations usually require that you be a member; information can be obtained directly from an association through the Internet, by telephone, or by mail.

Labor unions. Labor unions provide various employment services to members and potential members, including apprenticeship programs that teach a specific trade or skill. Contact the appropriate labor union or State apprenticeship council for more information.

State employment service offices. The State employment service, sometimes called the Job Service, operates in coordination with the U.S. Department of Labor's Employment and Training Administration. Local offices, found nationwide, help job seekers to find jobs and help employers to find qualified workers at no cost to either. To find the office nearest you, look in the State government telephone listings under "Job Service" or "Employment."

ADVERTISING, MARKETING, PROMOTIONS, PUBLIC RELATIONS, AND SALES MANAGER JOBS

Job matching and referral. At the State employment service office, an interviewer will determine if you are "job ready" or if you need help from counseling and testing services to assess your occupational aptitudes and interests and to help you choose and prepare for a career. After you are job ready, you may examine available job listings and select openings that interest you. A staff member can then describe the job openings in detail and arrange for interviews with prospective employers.

Services for special groups. By law, veterans are entitled to priority job placement at State employment service centers. If you are a veteran, a veterans' employment representative can inform you of available assistance and help you to deal with problems.

State employment service offices also refer people to opportunities available under the Workforce Investment Act (WIA) of 1998. Educational and career services and referrals are provided to employers and job seekers, including adults, dislocated workers, and youth. These programs help to prepare people to participate in the State's workforce, increase their employment and earnings potential, improve their educational and occupational skills, and reduce their dependency on welfare.

Federal Government. Information on obtaining a position with the Federal Government is available from the U.S. Office of Personnel Management (OPM) through USAJOBS, the Federal Government's official employment information system. This resource for locating and applying for job opportunities can be accessed through the Internet at http://www.usajobs.opm.gov or through an interactive voice response telephone system at (703) 724-1850 or TDD (978) 461-8404. These numbers are not toll free, and charges may result.

Community agencies. Many nonprofit organizations, including religious institutions and vocational rehabilitation agencies, offer counseling, career development, and job placement services, generally targeted to a particular group, such as women, youths, minorities, ex-offenders, or older workers.

Private employment agencies and career consultants. Private agencies can save you time and they will contact employers who otherwise might be difficult to locate. But these agencies may charge for their services. Most operate on a commission basis, charging a percentage of the first-year salary paid to a successful applicant. You or the hiring company will pay the fee. Find out the exact cost and who is responsible for paying associated fees before using the service. When determining if the service is worth the cost, consider any guarantees that the agency offers.

Internships. Many people find jobs with business and organizations with whom they have interned or volunteered. Look for internships and volunteer opportunities on job boards, career centers, and company and association Web sites, but also check community service organizations and volunteer opportunity databases. Some internships and long-term volunteer positions come with stipends and all provide experience and the chance to meet employers and other good networking contacts.

Applying for a Job

After you have found some jobs that interest you, the next step is to apply for them. You will almost always need to complete resumes or application forms and cover letters. Later, you will probably need to go on interviews to meet with employers face to face.

Resumes and application forms. Resumes and application forms give employers written evidence of your qualifications and skills. The goal of these documents is to prove—as clearly and directly as possible—how your qualifications match the job's requirements. Do this by highlighting the experience, accomplishments, education, and skills that most closely fit the job you want.

Gathering information. Resumes and application forms both include the same information. As a first step, gather the following facts:

- Contact information, including your name, mailing address, e-mail address (if you have one you check often), and telephone number.
- Type of work or specific job you are seeking or a qualifications summary, which describes your best skills and experience in just a few lines.

- Education, including school name and its city and State, months and years of attendance, highest grade completed or diploma or degree awarded, and major subject or subjects studied. Also consider listing courses and awards that might be relevant to the position. Include a grade point average if you think it would help in getting the job.
- Experience, paid and volunteer. For each job, include the job title, name and location of employer, and dates of employment. Briefly describe your job duties and major accomplishments. In a resume, use phrases instead of sentences to describe your work; write, for example, "Supervised 10 children" instead of writing "I supervised 10 children."
- Special skills. You might list computer skills, proficiency in foreign languages, achievements, or and membership in organizations in a separate section.
- References. Be ready to provide references if requested. Good references could be former employers, coworkers, or teachers or anyone else who can describe your abilities and job-related traits. You will be asked to provide

contact information for the people
you choose.

Throughout the application or resume, focus on
accomplishments that relate most closely to
the job you want. You can even use the job
announcement as a guide, using some of the
same words and phrases to describe your work
and education.

Look for concrete examples that show your
skills. When describing your work experience,
for instance, you might say that you increased
sales by 10 percent, finished a task in half the
usual time, or received three letters of
appreciation from customers.

Choosing a format. After gathering the
information you want to present, the next step
is to put it in the proper format. In an
application form, the format is set. Just fill in
the blanks. But make sure you fill it out
completely and follow all instructions. Do not
omit any requested information. Consider
making a copy of the form before filling it out,
in case you make a mistake and have to start
over. If possible, have someone else look over
the form before submitting it.

In a resume, there are many ways of
organizing the information you want to include,
but the most important information should
usually come first. Most applicants list their
past jobs in reverse chronological order,

describing their most recent employment first and working backward. But some applicants use a functional format, organizing their work experience under headings that describe their major skills. They then include a brief work history section that lists only job titles, employers, and dates of employment. Still other applicants choose a format that combines these two approaches in some way. Choose the style that best showcases your skills and experience.

Whatever format you choose, keep your resume short. Many experts recommend that new workers use a one-page resume. Avoid long blocks of text and italicized material. Consider using bullets to highlight duties or key accomplishments.

Before submitting your resume, make sure that it is easy to read. Are the headings clear and consistently formatted with bold or some other style of type? Is the type face large enough? Then, ask at least two people to proofread the resume for spelling and other errors and make sure you use your computer's spell checker.

Keep in mind that many employers scan resumes into databases, which they then search for specific keywords or phrases. The keywords are usually nouns referring to experience, education, personal characteristics, or industry buzz words. Identify keywords by reading the job description and qualifications in the job ad; use these same words in your resume. For example, if the job description includes customer service tasks, use the words "customer service" on your resume. Scanners sometimes misread paper resumes, which could mean some of your keywords don't get into the database. So, if you know that your resume will be scanned, and you have the option, e-mail an electronic version. If you must submit a paper resume, make it scannable by using a simple font and avoiding underlines, italics, and graphics. It is also a good idea to send a traditionally formatted resume along with your scannable resume, with a note on each marking its purpose.

Cover letters. When sending a resume, most people include a cover letter to introduce themselves to the prospective employer. Most cover letters are no more than three short paragraphs. Your cover letter should capture the employer's attention, follow a business letter format, and usually should include the following information:

- Name and address of the specific person to whom the letter is addressed.
- Reason for your interest in the company or position.
- Your main qualifications for the position.
- Request for an interview.

- Your home and work telephone numbers.

If you send a scannable resume, you should also include a scannable cover letter, which avoids graphics, fancy fonts, italics, and underlines.

As with your resume, it may be helpful to look for examples on the Internet or in books at your local library or bookstore, but be sure not to copy letters directly from other sources.

Job Interview Tips

An interview gives you the opportunity to showcase your qualifications to an employer, so it pays to be well prepared. The following information provides some helpful hints.

Preparation:

- Learn about the organization.
- Have a specific job or jobs in mind.
- Review your qualifications for the job.
- Be ready to briefly describe your experience, showing how it relates it the job.
- Be ready to answer broad questions, such as "Why should I hire you?" "Why do you want this job?" "What are your strengths and weaknesses?"
- Practice an interview with a friend or relative.

Personal appearance:

- Be well groomed.
- Dress appropriately.
- Do not chew gum or smoke.

The interview:

- Be early.

- Learn the name of your interviewer and greet him or her with a firm handshake.
- Use good manners with everyone you meet.
- Relax and answer each question concisely.
- Use proper English—avoid slang.
- Be cooperative and enthusiastic.
- Use body language to show interest—use eye contact and don't slouch.
- Ask questions about the position and the organization, but avoid questions whose answers can easily be found on the company Web site.
- Also avoid asking questions about salary and benefits unless a job offer is made.
- Thank the interviewer when you leave and shake hands.
- Send a short thank you note.

Information to bring to an interview:

- Social Security card.
- Government-issued identification (driver's license).
- Resume or application. Although not all employers require a resume, you should be able to furnish the interviewer information

about your education, training, and previous employment.

- References. Employers typically require three references. Get permission before using anyone as a reference. Make sure that they will give you a good reference. Try to avoid using relatives as references.
- Transcripts. Employers may require an official copy of transcripts to verify grades, coursework, dates of attendance, and highest grade completed or degree awarded.

Evaluating a Job Offer

Once you receive a job offer, you must decide if you want the job. Fortunately, most organizations will give you a few days to accept or reject an offer.

There are many issues to consider when assessing a job offer. Will the organization be a good place to work? Will the job be interesting? Are there opportunities for advancement? Is the salary fair? Does the employer offer good benefits? Now is the time to ask the potential employer about these issues—and to do some checking on your own.

The organization. Background information on an organization can help you to decide whether it is a good place for you to work. Factors to consider include the organization's business or activity, financial condition, age, size, and location.

You generally can get background information on an organization, particularly a large organization, on its Internet site or by telephoning its public relations office. A public company's annual report to the stockholders tells about its corporate philosophy, history, products or services, goals, and financial status. Most government agencies can furnish reports that describe their programs and missions. Press releases, company newsletters or magazines, and recruitment brochures also can be useful. Ask the organization for any other items that might interest a prospective employee. If possible, speak to current or former employees of the organization.

Background information on the organization may be available at your public or school library. If you cannot get an annual report, check the library for reference directories that may provide basic facts about the company, such as earnings, products and services, and number of employees. Some directories widely available in libraries either in print or as online databases include:

- Dun & Bradstreet's Million Dollar Directory
- Standard and Poor's Register of Corporations
- Mergent's Industrial Review (formerly Moody's Industrial Manual)
- Thomas Register of American Manufacturers
- Ward's Business Directory

Stories about an organization in magazines and newspapers can tell a great deal about its successes, failures, and plans for the future. You can identify articles on a company by looking under its name in periodical or computerized indexes in libraries, or by using one of the Internet's search engines. However, it probably will not be useful to look back more than 2 or 3 years.

The library also may have government publications that present projections of growth for the industry in which the organization is classified. Long-term projections of employment and output for detailed industries, covering the entire U.S. economy, are developed by the Bureau of Labor Statistics and revised every 2 years. (See the Career Guide to Industries, online at www.bls.gov/oco/cg.) Trade magazines also may include articles on the trends for specific industries.

Career centers at colleges and universities often have information on employers that is not available in libraries. Ask a career center representative how to find out about a particular organization.

During your research consider the following questions:

- Does the organization's business or activity match your own interests and beliefs?

- It is easier to apply yourself to the work if you are enthusiastic about what the organization does.

- How will the size of the organization affect you?

Large firms generally offer a greater variety of training programs and career paths, more managerial levels for advancement, and better employee benefits than do small firms. Large employers also may have more advanced technologies. However, many jobs in large firms tend to be highly specialized.

Jobs in small firms may offer broader authority and responsibility, a closer working relationship with top management, and a chance to clearly see your contribution to the success of the organization.

Should you work for a relatively new organization or one that is well established?

New businesses have a high failure rate, but for many people, the excitement of helping to create a company and the potential for sharing in its success more than offset the risk of job loss. However, it may be just as exciting and rewarding to work for a young firm that already has a foothold on success.

The job. Even if everything else about the job is attractive, you will be unhappy if you dislike the day-to-day work. Determining in advance whether you will like the work may be difficult. However, the more you find out about the job before accepting or rejecting the offer, the more likely you are to make the right choice. Consider the following questions:

Where is the job located?

If the job is in another section of the country, you need to consider the cost of living, the availability of housing and transportation, and the quality of educational and recreational facilities in that section of the country. Even if the job location is in your area, you should consider the time and expense of commuting.

Does the work match your interests and make good use of your skills?

 The duties and responsibilities of the job should be explained in enough detail to answer this question.

How important is the job to the company or organization?

An explanation of where you fit in the organization and how you are supposed to contribute to its overall goals should give you an idea of the job's importance.

What will the hours be?

Most jobs involve regular hours—for example, 40 hours a week, during the day, Monday through Friday. Other jobs require night, weekend, or holiday work. In addition, some jobs routinely require overtime to meet deadlines or sales or production goals, or to better serve customers. Consider the effect that the work hours will have on your personal life.

How long do most people who enter this job stay with the company?

High turnover can mean dissatisfaction with the nature of the work or something else about the job.

Opportunities offered by employers. A good job offers you opportunities to learn new skills, increase your earnings, and rise to positions of greater authority, responsibility, and prestige. A lack of opportunities can dampen interest in the work and result in frustration and boredom.

The company should have a training plan for you. What valuable new skills does the company plan to teach you?

The employer should give you some idea of promotion possibilities within the organization. What is the next step on the career ladder? If you have to wait for a job to become vacant before you can be promoted, how long does this usually take? When opportunities for advancement do arise, will you compete with applicants from outside the company? Can you apply for jobs for which you qualify elsewhere within the organization, or is mobility within the firm limited?

Salaries and benefits. When an employer makes a job offer, information about earnings and benefits are usually included. You will want to research to determine if the offer is fair. If you choose to negotiate for higher pay and better benefits, objective research will help you strengthen your case.

You should also look for additional information, specifically tailored to your job offer and circumstances. Try to find family, friends, or acquaintances who recently were hired in similar jobs. Ask your teachers and the staff in placement offices about starting pay for graduates with your qualifications. Help-wanted ads in newspapers sometimes give salary ranges for similar positions. Check the library or your school's career center for salary surveys such as those conducted by the National Association of Colleges and Employers or various professional associations.

If you are considering the salary and benefits for a job in another geographic area, make allowances for differences in the cost of living, which may be significantly higher in a large metropolitan area than in a smaller city, town, or rural area.

You also should learn the organization's policy regarding overtime. Depending on the job, you may or may not be exempt from laws requiring the employer to compensate you for overtime. Find out how many hours you will be expected to work each week and whether you receive overtime pay or compensatory time off for working more than the specified number of hours in a week.

Also take into account that the starting salary is just that—the start. Your salary should be reviewed on a regular basis; many organizations do it every year. How much can you expect to earn after 1, 2, or 3 or more years? An employer cannot be specific about the amount of pay if it includes commissions and bonuses.

Benefits also can add a lot to your base pay, but they vary widely. Find out exactly what the benefit package includes and how much of the cost you must bear.

WHAT TO EXPECT FROM THE OTHER SIDE OF THE TABLE...HIRING THE BEST ADVERTISING, MARKETING, PROMOTIONS, PUBLIC RELATIONS, AND SALES MANAGERS

This chapter is all about clarity of the total hiring process – for you, your manager and your candidates.

You will need or encounter a Great Process to Hire the Best. Computers and equipment are wonderful tools, but people make the difference. Hiring the Best makes it clear just how valuable it is to hire and work with the best. The mistakes you will avoid make the investment very valuable. Hiring the Best provides you with a process that reduces trial and error in recruiting a lot, but still ensures that you will be able to hire the best.

This chapter guides you to how to perform a truly in-depth hiring process and interview for candidates. The process will allow you and your company to select the best candidates for key positions.

You will be able to use the materials shown here as an outstanding tool, giving you insight into the candidates experience, performance history, and growth allowing you to determine what they are capable of today and in the future.

This will, in short, let you go from hoping your next hire works out to being confident your next hire will be a star.

Before you make your next hire, use this Guide.

THE INTERVIEW AND SELECTION PROCESS

A position description, observing the job being performed, and interviewing the previous and current holders of the job and the immediate supervisor will be helpful in determining the competencies required and the performance standard.

Asking a series of questions will help you in establishing the technical competencies. Ask questions such as:

- What would the "perfect" candidate's competencies and skills look like;
- What will a person in this job have to do on a regular basis to succeed;
- What are the necessary competencies and skills the person will need in order to achieve the desired results of the position;
- How will a person hired for this job know he or she is succeeding, and
- Why have people left this job in the past?

After you have analyzed the job and developed several technical competencies, list the top five most important technical competencies the candidate MUST have to succeed in the job. Remember when developing your interview questions to keep the questions open-ended, simple, direct and specific. Base all the questions on the job description and the top five technical competencies.

Avoid questions that require overly specific knowledge.

Below is a sample Technical Competency Assessment Guide for use in determining the technical competencies and developing relevant interview questions.

TECHNICAL COMPENTENCIES ASSESSMENT GUIDE

Job Title:

_____

A. Analyze Technical Aspects of Job. (Answer questions and list competencies in the space.)

- What would the "perfect" candidate's competencies and skills look like?

- What will a person in this job have to do on a regular basis to succeed?

- What are the necessary competencies and skills the person will need in order to achieve the desired results of the position?

- How will a person hired for this job know he or she is succeeding?

- Why have people left this job in the past?

B. List the top five most important technical competencies the candidate MUST have to succeed in the job.

1.

2.

3.

4.

5.

C. Develop a Technical Question for Each of the Five Required Technical Competencies.

- Base all your questions on the job description and the technical competencies you listed above.

- Keep the questions open-ended, simple, direct and specific.

- Avoid questions that require a specific knowledge of your division.

- Ask for assistance developing technical questions if you are not the technical expert.

Step 2

Determine the Customer Service Focused Competencies of the Job

A large percentage of employees who did not succeed in a position had the technical skills but did not have the customer service focused skills required for the job. Identifying the customer service focused competencies needed to successfully perform the job and determining if the candidate possesses those competencies is critical. For example, an individual working in a receptionist position will need to be flexible and unflappable in order to handle the pressure of multiple phone calls and simultaneous visitors. They also need some degree of friendliness for welcoming the public and some degree of extroversion, since most people calling an organization would like to be met by someone with enthusiasm.

Assessing customer service focused competencies during the interview process is something we may not be typically used to doing as managers. We are experienced in determining if the candidate has the technical skills and abilities to perform the job. But in order to get the BEST candidate for the position, customer service focused competencies need to be determined and assessed also.

To determine what customer service focused competencies are needed for the position, questions similar to those asked to determine the technical competencies should be answered:

- What would the "perfect" candidate's customer service focused competencies look like;
- What will a person in this job have to do on a regular basis to succeed;
- What are the necessary customer service focused competencies the person will need in order to achieve the desired results of the position;
- How will a person hired for this job know he or she is meeting the customer service focused expectations; and
- Related to customer service reasons, why have people left this job in the past?

As you think about the job vacancy you need to fill, focus on the customer service focused competencies or behaviors that an individual needs to exhibit in order to succeed in this job. Depending on the specific job under consideration, customer service focused characteristics, such as paying attention to detail, being self-motivated, getting along with others, having leadership qualities, and being tolerant of stressful events, are examples of the skills critical to success on the job.

Below you will find five descriptive elements of personality to assist you in determining customer service focused competencies. Descriptive words have been added to give you ideas and help you determine what behaviors are required for the position.

Towards the end of this document, you will find a list of questions to correspond to each personality factor. These questions can be used to develop the examination portion of the recruiting announcement or they can be used in the interview process.

The five descriptive elements of personality are Responsible, Likeable, Believable, Outgoing and Unflappable.

Definitions:

Responsible. The ability to organize or schedule people, tasks, and self; to develop realistic action plans while remaining sensitive to time constraints and resource availability; and having a well developed sense of ethics and integrity. Characterized by high levels of responsibility and behaviors these employees are controlled, disciplined, precise, persistent, and businesslike. Their behavior is consistent, scrupulous, and reliable, and their work is purposeful, highly systematic, and well organized. They approach life as a series of tasks to be accomplished and goals to be reached.

Descriptors: detail-oriented; quality-focused; high-integrity; responsible; trustworthy; dependable; cost-conscious; exact; disciplined; committed; cautious; casual; easygoing.

Likeable. Describes a person's ability to modify their behavioral style to respond to the needs of others while maintaining one's own objectives and sense of dignity. In the moderate to high range of likeability, we find sympathetic, helpful, and understanding individuals. They are agreeable, compassionate, thoughtful, and kind. They appear to accept things as they are, nurture others, and are obviously friendly and caring people.

Descriptors: amicable; accommodating; supportive; helpful; compromising; collaborative; friendly; empathetic; empowering; congenial; easygoing.

Believable. Capable of eliciting belief or trust. In the middle to low range of believable thinking, we find people who are open, willing to reexamine tenets and consider new ideas. They are capable of reasonable levels of professional and personal risk taking and are willing to work outside their "comfort zone." Highly believable people can be described as practical, predictable and conventional, willing to follow procedures without question. They often form the emotional "back bone" of an organization.

Descriptors: creative; original; flexible; spontaneous; open-to-new-ideas; independent; curious; untraditional; venturesome; uninhibited; conventional; down-to-earth; concrete; traditional; practical; methodical; systematic.

Outgoing. Describes the ability to work with people in such a manner as to build high morale and group commitments to goals and objectives. Individuals in the moderately high range of extroversion are upbeat, positive, and energetic. They tend to be enterprising, cheerful, and appropriately assertive. They demonstrate leadership, team-building capability, and are able to coach or facilitate a work team's progress. Individuals who are moderately introverted are often viewed as self-contained, generally well balanced, and able to work well either alone or in small groups.

Descriptors: active; outgoing; dominant; forceful; enthusiastic; assertive; persuasive; energizing; entrepreneurial; ambitious; risk-taking; self-contained; task-oriented; quiet; restrained; formal; unassuming; reserved; thoughtful.

Unflappable. The ability to maintain a mature, problem-solving attitude while dealing with a range of stressful conditions, such as interpersonal conflict, hazardous conditions, personal rejection, hostility, or time demands. At moderately high levels of stress tolerance we find relaxed, secure, and hardy individuals who are poised and adaptive in a wide range of situations. They are steady, realistic, self-reliant, and able to cope effectively across a wide range of situations and circumstances. They demonstrate maturity that is not necessarily related to age, but to the ability to maintain a clear perspective under stressful conditions as well as those that elicit little or no stress.

Descriptors: calm; well adjusted; secure; even-tempered; self-assured; unflappable; resilient; poised; composed; self-confident; optimistic.

CUSTOMER SERVICE FOCUSED BEHAVIORS ASSESSMENT GUIDE

Job Title:

_____

A. List the most typical Customer Service Focused behaviors required on this job on a daily basis. Use the previously identified personality factors to help you.

Responsible – detail-oriented; quality-focused; high-integrity; responsible; trustworthy; dependable; cost conscious; exact; disciplined; committed; cautious; casual; easygoing.

Likeable – amicable; accommodating; supportive; helpful; compromising; collaborative; friendly; empathetic; empowering; congenial; easygoing.

Believable – creative; original; flexible; spontaneous; open-to-new-ideas; independent; curious; untraditional; venturesome; uninhibited; conventional; down-to-earth; concrete; traditional; practical; methodical; systematic.

Outgoing – active; outgoing; dominant; forceful; enthusiastic; assertive; persuasive; energizing; entrepreneurial; ambitious; risk-taking; self-contained; task-oriented; quiet; restrained; formal; unassuming; reserved; thoughtful.

Unflappable – calm; well-adjusted; secure; even-tempered; self-assured; unflappable; resilient; poised; composed; self-confident; optimistic.

B. List of Customer Service Focused Behaviors
   1.

   2.

   3.

   4.

   5.

**C. Develop a Question for Each of the
Customer Service Focused Behaviors**
   1.

   2.

   3.

   4.

   5.

Step 3

**Develop Interview Questions to Assess
Both Technical and Customer Service
Focused Competencies**

Decide how long the interviews will be and
select a reasonable number of questions to
ask. In a half-hour interview, only about 5
behavioral-based questions can comfortably be

asked. If five questions are asked, at least two of them should be customer service-type questions, depending upon the type of job.

Always ask open-ended questions. Ask, *"This job involves dealing with difficult customers. Think of a time when you had to deal with a difficult customer and tell us what you did."* Don't ask, *"Have you ever dealt with difficult customers?"* You probably will get an answer like, "Yes, I work with difficult customers all the time." But it won't tell you HOW the individual works with difficult customers. If you feel the candidate is making up an answer, or is giving you a "canned" answer, ask a probing question or two to get more detail. *"What exactly did you say to the customer to get them to stop yelling."* Generally, if they have read a book on "most commonly asked interview questions" and memorized an answer, or are making up the situation, a probing question will generally fluster them and they will not be as confident in giving an answer. You can ask for the candidate to think of another example to use in answering the question.

Using the list of most important tasks you developed during the review of the Position Description, develop open-ended questions to determine if the candidate has the technical skills necessary for the job. Only ask technical questions that relate to that particular job.

Don't ask a question about using equipment if they don't use that equipment to do their job.

Using the list of customer service focused skills you identified from the position description are needed to do the job, develop open-ended questions to determine the candidate's customer service focused competencies.

There is a list of sample interview questions at the end of this document to help you.

They are arranged by the five personality factors identified above.

Step 4

Conducting the Interview
Have an interview panel of at least two managers/supervisors; some managers may also wish to include a non-management employee with special knowledge of the position duties as part of a panel.

If you choose to include a non-management employee on your interview panel, be sure to discuss interviewing procedures and confidentiality of candidate information with the employee prior to the interviews. It is encouraged that all interview panels be as diverse as possible.

Before the interview starts, establish the criteria used for scoring and then meet with the interview panel to discuss the process and review the questions and criteria used for scoring.

Welcome the candidate and establish rapport by introducing them to the members of the interview panel. Ask easy questions such as "Did you have any difficulty finding the office?" or "Would you like a glass of water before we begin?" Give a brief explanation of the organization or section and show the organization chart so they understand how this position fits within the organization. If you have handed the position description and organization chart out while they waited for the interview to start, ask if they have any questions about the position or organization. Explaining the interview process can also help ease a candidate's nervousness and also gives them information about the process, including, approximate length of the interview, the interview will be a series of prepared questions asked by the interview panel designed to get to know the candidate, and the panel will be taking notes during the interview.

Transition into the main purpose of the interview by saying, "Let's get a bit more focused and start asking the interview questions." Even though the interview process is accomplished through a panel, one person should act as "facilitator" and make sure the interview stays focused. Some candidates tend to wander, give "canned" speeches, or simply try to deliver a monologue. In such cases, you need to diplomatically interrupt and redirect the candidate to the question at hand. You might simply say, "I think we've gotten a little off target here. Let me restate my question."

To clarify a response or to get a candidate to give specific examples you can ask, "Please give me a specific example about when you..." Because behavior-based questions require specific examples to answer them successfully, sometimes a candidate will need to think for a few seconds to come up with an appropriate example. You may have to wait 30, 60, or even 90 seconds for the candidate to start answering the question. Resist the temptation to talk during this silence! It takes time to recall specific behavioral examples that clearly answer your questions and you want the candidate to do their best during the interview. An option available to the hiring manager is to hand out the list of questions to the candidates a few minutes before the interview starts, so the candidate can start thinking of specific examples ahead of time and organizing their thoughts.

If an answer does not give you the information you need to rate the candidate's answer, use open-ended probes such as:

"Could you review your role in..."
"Please describe how you..."
"What happened after..."

If after the first or second try to get an answer more relevant to the question move on to the next question.

After each interview take a few minutes for the panel members to summarize their thoughts and score the questions, or complete the rating process.

Affirmative Action

Organizations value diversity in the workplace. Every effort will be made to reach out to the broadest possible labor market. All employment decisions will be based on the most suitable candidate relative to a position, while taking into consideration Affirmative Action goals.

Step 5

Background and Reference Checks

The final stage of the hiring process is the background and reference checks. The Human Resources Background Investigator will verify information provided by the applicant by contacting former and current supervisors, persons listed by the candidate as references, and others who are thought to be able to provide information about the competencies of a candidate.

The Background Investigator listens for subtle innuendoes and long pauses after posing questions, and will evaluate whether the individual giving the reference sounds like he/she is struggling to carefully select each word. In these instances, more specific probing questions will be asked.

Occasionally, a finalist will indicate they do not wish you to contact their current employer. In these cases, you need to explain that the organization needs to contact this employer to assist with the hiring decision and that we don't hire anyone without completing a background and reference check with the current employer.

Making a Job Offer

When you have identified the candidate to whom you would like to make a job offer based on the information gathered through the application, examination, interview, evaluation of background and references, and you have the approval of your supervisor, and the Director or Deputy Director, you may contact that candidate and offer him/her the position.

Before you contact the candidate, please work closely with Human Resources staff to verify certain information. For example,
Classification
Salary Range
Rate of pay and timing of first pay increase

Vacation accrual rate and ability to transfer
vacation accruals from another State
organization
Trial Service period
Eligibility for Personal benefits

Confirming Job Offer Letter

Human Resources staff will send a confirming
job offer letter. The letter will outline the
terms of the job offer and will provide a space
for the candidate to sign his or her name
confirming that he/she accepts the terms of
employment. This signed copy must be
returned to Human Resources to document the
understanding and the acceptance of the
terms.
It is important that all information in this letter
of confirming letter of hire be correctly stated
because it is an implied employment contract.

Informing Unsuccessful Candidates

After the selected candidate formally accepts
your job offer, each of the remaining
candidates should be contacted to notify them
that the hiring decision has been made.
Human Resources can help you with this step.

If a candidate contacts you directly to ask why
he or she was not hired, the best thing to do is
to simply tell them that we hired the most
suitable candidate for the position. If they
continue to ask for information, contact your

Human Resources staff for guidance in how to answer the candidate's questions.

Retention of Interview Materials

Please collect all interview and selection materials and notes and return them promptly to Human Resources.

ADVERTISING, MARKETING, PROMOTIONS, PUBLIC RELATIONS, AND SALES MANAGER JOBS

SAMPLE CUSTOMER SERVICE FOCUSED INTERVIEW QUESTIONS

(Grouped by customer service based behaviors)

Responsible

1 Tell us about a time when the details of something you were doing were especially important. How did you attend to them?

2 Describe a time when you had to make a difficult decision on the job. What facts did you consider? How long did it take you to make a decision?

3 Jobs differ in the extent to which people work independently or as part of a team. Tell us about a time when you worked independently.

4 It is often easy to blur the distinction between confidential information and public knowledge. Have you ever been faced with this dilemma? What did you do?

5 Tell us about a time when you put in some extra effort to help move a particular project forward. How did you do it and what happened?

6 Tell us about a demanding situation in which you managed to remain calm and composed. What did you do and what was the outcome?

7 There are times when we have a great deal of paperwork to complete in a short

time. How do you do to ensure your accuracy?

8 Give an example of a time you noticed a process or task that was not being done correctly. How did you discover or come to notice it, and what did you do?

9 We often have to push ourselves harder to reach a target. Give us a specific example of when you had to give yourself that extra push.

10 Tell us about a time when you achieved success through your willingness to react quickly.

11 Tell us about a time when you disagreed with a procedure or policy instituted by management. What was your reaction and how did you implement the procedure or policy?

12 What kinds of measures have you taken to make sure all of the small details of a project or assignment were done? Please give a specific example.

13 How do you determine what constitutes a top priority in scheduling your work? Give a specific example.

14 If I call your references, what will they say about you?

15 What are two or three examples of tasks that you do not particularly enjoy doing? Tell us how you remain motivated to complete those tasks.

16 What has been your greatest success, personally or professionally?

17 What can you tell us about yourself that you feel is unique and makes you the best candidate for this position?

18 What strengths do you have that we haven't talked about?

19 Tell us about a time when you had to review detailed reports or documents to identify a problem. How did you go about it? What did you do when you discovered a problem?

20 How do you determine what constitutes a top priority in scheduling your time (the time of others)?

21 Do you have a system for organizing your own work area? Tell us how that system helped you on the job.

22 Have you planned any conferences, workshops or retreats? What steps did you take to plan the event?

Likeable

1 Tell us about a time when you were able to build a successful relationship with a difficult person.

2 Give us an example of how you have been able to develop a close, positive relationship with one of your customers.

3 Give us an example of how you establish an atmosphere at work where others feel comfortable in communicating their ideas, feelings and concerns.

4 Describe a particularly trying customer complaint or resistance you had to handle. How did you react and what was the outcome?

5 How would you describe your management style? How do you think your subordinates perceive you?

6 Some people are difficult to work with. Tell us about a time when you encountered such a person. How did you handle it?

7 In working with people, we find that what works with one person does not work with another. Therefore, we have to be flexible in our style of relating to others. Give us a specific example of when you had to vary your work style with a particular individual. How did it work out?

8 It is important to remain composed at work and to maintain a positive outlook. Give us a specific example of when you were able to do this.

9 Having an understanding of the other person's perspective is crucial in dealing with customers. Give us an example of a time when you achieved success through attaining insight into the other person's perspective.

10 Have you ever had difficulty getting along with a co-worker? How did you handle the situation and what was the outcome?

11 Tell us about a time when you needed someone's cooperation to complete a task and the person was uncooperative. What did you do? What was the outcome?

12 There are times when people need extra assistance with difficult projects. Give us an example of when you offered assistance to someone with whom you worked.

13 Tell us about a situation in which you became frustrated or impatient when dealing with a coworker. What did you do? What was the outcome?

14 Many jobs are team-oriented where a work group is the key to success. Give us an example of a time when you worked on a team to complete a project. How did it work? What was the outcome?

15 Tell us about a job where the atmosphere was the easiest for you to get along and function well. Describe the qualities of that work environment.

responsibilities. Tell what you did and us about a time when this happened.

10 What are your standards of success in your job and how do you know when you are successful?

11 Sometimes supervisors' evaluations differ from our own. What did you do about it?

12 What do you do differently from other (_____)? Why? Give examples.

13 We don't always make decisions that everyone agrees with. Give us an example of an unpopular decision you made. How did you communicate the decision and what was the outcome?

14 Describe a situation in which you received a new procedure or instructions with which you disagreed. What did you do?

15 Describe a situation in which you had to translate a broad or general directive from superiors into individual performance expectations. How did you do this and what were the results?

16 Give an example of how you monitor the progress your employees are making on projects or tasks you delegated.

Outgoing

1 Describe a time when you were able to effectively communicate a difficult or unpleasant idea to a superior.

2 Tell us about a time when you had to motivate a group of people to get an important job done. What did you do, what was the outcome?

3 Tell us about a time when you delayed responding to a situation until you had time to review the facts, even though there was pressure to act quickly.

4 There are times when we need to insist on doing something a certain way. Give us the details surrounding a situation when you had to insist on doing something "your way". What was the outcome?

5 On occasion, we have to be firm and assertive in order to achieve a desired result. Tell us about a time when you had to do that.

6 Being successful is hard work. Tell us about a specific achievement when you had to work especially hard to attain the success you desired.

7 In job situations you may be pulled in many different directions at once. Tell us about a time when you had to respond to this type of situation. How did you manage yourself?

8 Many of us have had co-workers or managers who tested our patience. Tell us about a time when you restrained

yourself to avoid conflict with a co-worker or supervisor. (restrained)

9 In working with people, we find that what works with one person does not work with another. Therefore, we have to be flexible in our style of relating to others. Give us a specific example of when you had to vary your work style with a particular individual. How did it work out?

10 Describe some particularly trying customer complaints or resistance you have had to handle. How did you react? What was the outcome?

11 Have you ever had difficulty getting along with co-workers? How did you handle the situation and what was the outcome?

12 Tell us about a time when you needed someone's cooperation to complete a task and the person was uncooperative. What did you do? What was the outcome?

13 Tell us about a situation in which you became frustrated or impatient when dealing with a coworker. What did you do? What was the outcome?

14 Sooner or later we all have to deal with a customer who has unreasonable demands. Think of a time when you had to handle unreasonable requests. What did you do and what was the outcome?

15 Tell us about a time when you were effective in handling a customer complaint. Why were you effective? What was the outcome?

16 How do you know if your customers are satisfied?

Unflappable

1 There are times when we all have to deal with deadlines and it can be stressful. Tell us about a time when you felt pressured at work and how you coped with it.

2 Give us an example of a demanding situation when you were able to maintain your composure while others got upset.

3 On occasion, we experience conflict with our superiors. Describe such a situation and tell us how you handled the conflict. What was the outcome?

4 We have to find ways to tolerate and work with difficult people. Tell us about a time when you have done this.

5 Many times, a job requires you to quickly shift your attention from one task to the next. Tell us about a time at work when you had to change focus onto another task. What was the outcome?

6 Tell us about a time when you received accurate, negative feedback by a co-worker, boss, or customer. How did you handle the evaluation? How did it affect your work?

7 Give us an example of when you felt overly sensitive to feedback or criticism. How did you handle your feelings?

8 Give us an example of when you made a presentation to an uninterested or hostile audience. How did it turn out?

9 Tell us about a time when you put in some extra effort to help move a project

forward. How did you do that? What happened?

10 Describe suggestions you have made to improve work procedures. How did it turn out?

ADVERTISING, MARKETING, PROMOTIONS, PUBLIC RELATIONS, AND SALES MANAGER JOBS

INTERVIEWING

A Practical Guide for Selecting

THE INTERVIEW PROCESS

1.   PLANNING

Time spent planning will ensure the interview process proceeds smoothly and that you obtain the information needed to assess the candidates. You should:

- Review the position description and qualification requirements (refer to the vacancy announcement).

- Thoroughly review all candidate applications. Ask yourself: – What are the strengths/weaknesses of this candidate?

- What is the candidate's relevant skills/experience? – Does the education fit the job requirements?

- Is there evidence of the ability to communicate with individuals and groups from diverse backgrounds in a variety of situations?

- Is there evidence of the ability to lead and accomplish work through others?

- Decide who you will interview. Although you are not required to interview all candidates, think about the perception of other candidates if you interview only one person.

- Formulate questions and write them down. This will help ensure you ask all candidates the same questions.

- Allow 1-2 hours for the interview.

2. CONFIRMING/SCHEDULING INTERVIEW

Selecting officials are encouraged to confirm scheduled interviews with applicants in writing.

3. CONDUCTING THE INTERVIEW

After welcoming the candidate, spend a few minutes chatting informally. It will help you both relax.

- Give a **brief overview** of the job and mission of the organization.

- Ask questions and listen.

- Probe for additional information. Ask the candidate to elaborate on or clarify what was just said. (Although it is important that you write down a list of questions before you begin the interviews, you are not prohibited from asking additional questions.)

Indirect probing is also an effective way to elicit more information. If you are silent for a few seconds after the candidate responds, that may allow them time to think of additional things to say; or you may use neutral phrases, such as: I see, or, oh? That may prompt the candidate to elaborate further. **The point is that in this phase of the interview, it is the candidate who should be doing most of the talking.**

- Take notes, but don't try to capture every word. It's distracting to you and the candidate.

- Allow the candidate time to ask questions. This is where you can elaborate on the Organization, your lab, and/or the specific job.

- Inform the candidate about maxi flex, leave, benefits, holidays, etc.

Some suggested interview questions can be found in Section III, TIPS ON INTERVIEWING.

4. CLOSING

If the candidate won't be considered further,
close the interview diplomatically. If you are
interested in the candidate, you may:

- Ask if the candidate is still interested in
  the position.

- Inform the candidate of the next step. Be
  prepared to advise on the timeframe for
  selection and how the selectee will be
  notified.

- Inform the candidate that references will
  be checked.

- Thank the candidate for coming for the
  interview, applying for the position,
  and/or having an interest in the
  Organization and position.

- Write up your notes.

5. FOLLOW-UP

A good customer service practice is to write
all candidates acknowledging the interview
and thanking the person for showing an
interest in the organization. You may wish to
do so after a selection has been made.

TIPS ON INTERVIEWING

1. QUESTIONS/ASSESSMENT TOOLS

Careful thought should be given to constructing the interview.

Together with the KSAs (knowledge, skills, and abilities) and SPFs (selective placement factors) you used in the vacancy announcement, the kind of questions you ask will determine the type of person you select for your position. There are various assessment tools available to evaluate candidates including:

A. The Behavioral Event Inventory (BEI). The candidate **describes, in detail, a past experience that demonstrates the KSA or competency to a panel.** The panel is facilitated by a person trained in the method. The phases of the process include planning, orientation, and interviewing, debriefing, and follow-up documentation.

B. The Traditional Interview. Questions are developed prior to the interview. The same basic questions are asked of each candidate. Additionally the interviewer can,
- Encourage the candidate to give an example of a real situation, activity, or problem that includes: a description of the context, or environment; evidence or characteristics of the audience; the

action taken; and the outcome.

- Ask open-ended questions. Asking yes and no questions will severely limit the kind of information you obtain from the interview. The only yes or no question you should ask is, "Are you still interested in this position?"

2. INTERVIEW QUESTIONS TO GET YOU STARTED

- What interests you most about our position?

- What role do you take in a group situation? Give an example.
- Why do you want to work for our organization?

- What are your short-term and long-term goals?

- What are the two biggest accomplishments in your life?

- What has been your greatest technical achievement in your current position? Your career?

- Describe your participation in professional associations.

- What planning processes have you

found useful? In what way do you feel you have improved in your planning abilities/methods?

- How does your past experience impact your qualifications for this position?

3. SUPERVISOR & MANAGER COMPETENCIES

When preparing for supervisory or managerial interviews (whether using traditional or BEI), all candidates must be evaluated using the following two competencies:

A. Leading People. This competency includes conflict management, cultural awareness, team building, mentoring, and integrity/honesty (either work related or outside experience). Ask each candidate to describe a situation, problem, or event that demonstrates:

- Ability to work with a diverse group.

- Ability to prevent or mediate a conflict or disagreement or overcome dissension in a group.

- Ability to instill trust and confidence in others.

- Use of skills and abilities as a leader under stressful conditions.

B. Building Coalitions/Communications.

This competency includes oral and/or written communication, influencing/negotiating, partnering, interpersonal skills, and political savvy. Ask each candidate to describe a situation, problem or event that demonstrates:

- Ability to express ideas or give instructions not easily or readily understood by their audience.

- Ability to make presentations to groups in order to gain acceptance of an idea by the group.

- Negotiating skills to gain approval for change or modification to programs, procedures, etc.

4. INTERVIEWING PEOPLE WITH DISABILITIES

Concentrate on the applicant's technical and professional knowledge, skills, abilities, experiences and interests, not on the disability. Remember, you cannot interview a disability, hire a disability or supervise a disability. You can interview a person, hire a person, and supervise a person.

The American with Disabilities Act (ADA)

separates the hiring process into three stages: **pre-offer, post-offer** and **employment**. At each stage, the rules differ regarding the permissibility of disability-related questions and medical examinations. Definition of a "Disability-Related Question" means a question that is likely to elicit information about the disability. Definition of "Medical Examination" is a procedure or test that seeks information about an individual's physical or mental impairments or health.

Therefore, the two most important questions for employers to address are:

- Is the question disability-related or is the examination medical? And

- Where are we (i.e., at which stage - pre-offer, post-offer, or employment) in the employment process?

At the first stage (the pre-offer stage), the ADA prohibits all disability-related questions and medical examinations, even if the questions or examinations are related to the job. At the second stage (after the applicant is given a conditional job offer), the law allows all disability-related questions and medical examinations, as long as all entering employees in the job category are asked the questions or given the examinations. At the third stage (after the employee starts work), the law permits disability-related questions and medical examinations only if they are job-related and consistent with business necessity.

The law requires that medical information collected at any stage must be kept confidential.

For examples of some commonly asked questions on "Pre-employment Disability - Related Questions and Medical Examination Questions," please refer to the Equal Employment Opportunity Commission website at www.eeoc.gov/docs/preemp.html.

5. ACCOMMODATING PERSONS WITH DISABILITIES FOR AN INTERVIEW

- Application and interviewing procedures should comply with the American with Disabilities Act (ADA). The ADA prohibits disability-related questions or medical exams before a real job offer is made.

- Agencies employment offices and interviewing location(s) are to be accessible to applicants with mobility, visual, hearing or cognitive disabilities.

- Be willing to make appropriate and

reasonable accommodations to enable a job applicant with a disability to present him or herself in the best possible light. When setting up the interview explain what the hiring process involves and ask the individual if he or she will need reasonable accommodations for any part of the interview process. For example, if a person who is blind states he or she will need help filling out forms, provide the assistance; provide an interpreter for an applicant who is deaf, if he or she requests one; provide details or specific instructions to applicants with cognitive disabilities, if this type of accommodation is required.

- Do not let a rehabilitation counselor, social worker or other third party take an active part in or sit in on an interview unless the applicant requests it.

- Make sure that all questions asked during the interview are job-related. Speak to essential job functions regarding the position for which the applicant is applying, as well as why, how, where, when and by whom each task or operation is performed. Do not ask whether or not the individual needs an accommodation to perform these functions, because such information is likely to reveal whether or not the

101

individual has a disability. This is an ADA requirement to ensure that an applicant with a disability in not excluded before a real job offer is made.

6.   INTERVIEW DOs & DON'Ts

DO...

- Be friendly to establish rapport, help the candidate feel at ease.

- Listen attentively.

- Keep the interview under control. If the interviewee becomes verbose or drifts off the subject, it's your job to get back on track.

- Use professional terminology to evaluate the candidate's knowledge.

- Consider potential as well as current ability.

- Note the kinds of questions the candidate asks. Do they concern opportunities for self-improvement and increased responsibilities, or only pay and fringe benefits?

- Be objective.   Know yourself and your stereotypes.

- Understand that we tend to hire people who look like us.

- Be honest, even if it means saying something negative (e.g., the facility is old and there is not much office space). Just don't overemphasize it.

- Observe the candidate.

- Relax and enjoy the interview.

DON'T...

- Talk too much.

- Use a rigid or overly standardized approach. If you've prepared your questions, you can be flexible during the interview, knowing that you can easily get back on track. You'll become more flexible and react easily to different situations and personalities as you gain experience.

- Try to impress the interviewee with your knowledge.

- Hide demands of the job. A good candidate reacts favorably to these.

- Make commitments you may regret or are not authorized to make.

- Be satisfied with surface facts. Look for reasons, and probe.

- Take detailed notes. It may keep you from observing nonverbal responses and maintaining the conversational flow.
- Ask questions in a way that indicates the answers you want.

- Ask convoluted or over-defined questions.

- Be aggressive or evasive.

- Raise candidates' hopes when they are not likely to be selected.

CHECKING REFERENCES

You have completed the interviews, but you are not done yet.

A resume and interview are great tools, but **the reference check is really the only way you have to verify information given by the candidates.**

Normally, you will conduct a reference check on the one or two finalists. Reliability of the reference check is based on the concept that past performance is a good predictor of future performance. Reference checks will help:

- Verify information the candidate provided both in the application and during the interview.

- You gain insight into who your candidates are and how they behave in the workplace.

Never make an offer (remember, you can only make a tentative offer) **without first doing an exhaustive check** of the candidate's background. A comprehensive reference check goes back 5 years and includes contacting a minimum of three sources that are knowledgeable about the candidate's abilities. Contact

Enough references to confirm the quality of

your selection.

1. WHICH REFERENCES SHOULD I CHECK?

- Academic references–institutions **and** teachers/professors.
- Current and former supervisors– immediate supervisors are often the best sources for reliable information about a candidate's work performance.

- Your network of professional associates/associations.

- Candidate's personal references–they will generally provide a favorable reference. Ask them for names and positions of other persons who know the candidate and contact them.

- Candidate's colleagues–business or work associates will sometimes provide an objective analysis of the candidate's strengths and weaknesses.

- Seek your own independent sources who know the candidate.

2. TIPS FOR CHECKING REFERENCES

- Ask only job-related questions and ask the same questions about each candidate.

- Ask open-ended questions and probe.

- Use telephone reference checks rather than mail inquiries since they are faster and less time consuming.

- Keep the conversation casual. If you speak to the person in a relaxed manner, you will get better results.
- If the reference provider keeps talking, keep listening and asking more questions. Seek out judgmental comments and try to read between the lines of what the person is telling you. A reference who says the candidate tried hard or is a people person may be saying such things to avoid talking about real problems or issues.

- Do not eliminate one candidate because of poor references and then neglect to check references from the remaining candidate(s).

- Always check dates and times the person giving the reference worked with or supervised the candidate, and then
- Determine if there is a personal relationship.

- Give only a general description of the vacant position. Too many details may bias the reference person in formulating their answers. As in the case of the employment interview, let the other person do most of the talking.

- Do not use leading questions such as "He's a good manager, isn't he?"

- Do not let a prominent characteristic, such as a good academic record; overshadow less obvious or possibly negative traits, such as a poor leave record.

- Speak to someone in addition to the current supervisor. A dishonest supervisor may try to unload a problem employee by giving a glowing reference.

- Listen carefully to the answers you are given and take notes.

3. THE REFERENCE CHECK: QUESTIONS TO ASK

When contacting a reference, we recommend you begin with,

"Thank you for taking a few moments to provide information about our job candidate. The information you provide will be considered along with other information submitted by the applicant and other references. Please be aware that under the

Federal government's employment policies, we may become obligated to disclose the information to the applicant or others involved in the selection or review process."

Then, ask and record the answers to the following:

- How long have you known the candidate?
- In what capacity were you associated with the candidate?

- As employer?   Supervisor? Co-worker? Friend?   Other?

- Using a scale of 1-5, with 1 being poor and 5 being excellent, how would you rate the candidate in comparison to most others you have known.

RATINGS

1 2 3 4 5

Work ethic?	_____
Work quality?	_____
Technical skills?	_____
Writing skills?	_____
Communication skills?	_____
Interpersonal skills?	_____
Reliability & dependability?	_____
Receptivity to feedback?	_____
Adaptability to change?	_____

109

Ability to deal with job stress?   _____

- What would you consider to be some of this candidate's most positive attributes or strengths?

- What would you consider to be some areas where this person is not as strong or needs to improve?

- What type of work environment does the candidate require to excel?

- Describe the candidate's initiative, personality, and negative habits.

- How does the candidate get along with customers? Co-workers? Supervisors and managers?

- Is the candidate reliable? Honest? Trustworthy? Of good character?

- Would you rehire the candidate?

- Is there any other information concerning the candidate's qualifications, character, conduct and general fitness I should know about?

PROHIBITED QUESTIONS & PRACTICES

Please do not put yourself in a position of

engaging in a prohibited personnel practice related to employment and selection. As a selecting official with the authority to take, direct others to take, recommend, or approve any personnel action, **you must not:**

- Discriminate for or against any employee or candidate for employment on the basis of race, color, national origin, gender, religion, age, disability, political beliefs, sexual orientation, and marital or family status.

- Deceive or willfully obstruct any person with respect to such person's right to compete for employment.

- Influence any person to withdraw from competition for any position for the purpose of improving or injuring the prospects of any other person for employment.

- Appoint or employ a relative to a position over which you exercise jurisdiction or control as a selecting official.

- Take or fail to take a personnel action with respect to a candidate for employment as a reprisal.

- Discriminate for or against a candidate

for employment on the basis of conduct which does not adversely affect the performance of the candidate or the performance of others (except for criminal behavior).

RECORDING A PROFILE OF IMPRESSIONS

Candidate's Name_____

1. What are the candidate's strongest assets in relation to the requirements for this position?

2. What are the candidate's shortcomings in relation to this position?

3. The candidate seemed knowledgeable about/ interested in:

4. Contradictions or inconsistencies noted were:

5. The candidate was evasive about:

6. Overall, the candidate responded to questions with: (e.g., openness, confidence, poise,

directness, glibness,
evasiveness, etc.) Examples?

7. Overall, reference checks were
positive, mediocre, less than positive.
Examples/key descriptions or
characteristics?

**SUPERVISORY & MANAGERIAL
COMPETENCIES:** Leading People is there
evidence demonstrating:

1. Ability to gain commitment and support
from others?

2. Ability to develop solutions to
management problems?

3. Ability to establish performance
objectives?

4. Ability to foster cooperative working
environment among employees?

5. Ability to deal with morale and employee
concerns?

Building Coalitions/Communication is there evidence demonstrating:

1. Conflict resolution?

2. Working as a member of a team?

3. Expression of ideas and views that others understand and that influence (persuade) them to act?

ADVERTISING, MARKETING, PROMOTIONS, PUBLIC RELATIONS, AND SALES MANAGER JOBS

RECRUITING ADMINISTRATIVE SERVICES MANAGER

It Takes More Than A Job Announcement!

One of the critical steps in the recruitment process involves the actions you take to speed up the process and reach the largest, desirable pool of candidates.

Simply posting the vacancy on job websites will not guarantee that you receive quality applications for the job. This chapter provides suggestions on steps **YOU** should take to ensure **YOUR** recruitment activity works for **YOU**.

Considering these suggestions can help minimize the time required for recruitment on **YOUR** end and also help the Human Resources (HR) Specialist speed up the process.

BEFORE SUBMITTING the Vacancy

- *REVIEW AND RETHINK THE POSITION DESCRIPTION*
  - Ensure that the duties and responsibilities reflect the needs (or discipline) of the position at this time.
  - Determine if it accurately reflects the knowledge, skills, and abilities (KSAs) needed to perform the job.

117

- o Ensure that the KSAs can be directly related back to duties and responsibilities in the position description.
- o Develop your "Quality Experience" definition. Identify experience a candidate will need to bring to the job on day one.
- **CONSIDER ALTERNATIVE HIRING METHODS**
  - o Determine if the position can be filled using the Student Career Experience Program (SCEP), Federal Career Intern Program, Career Enhancement Program, and USDA Direct Hire Authority, special hiring authorities for individuals with disabilities or veterans, or other hiring methods.
- **THINK ABOUT THE VACANCY ANNOUNCEMENT**
  - o Determine who the applicants are you are trying to reach.
  - o Determine if you will need to recruit nationwide or if there will be sufficient candidates in the local commuting area to give you a diverse applicant pool from which to select.
- **DEVELOP A STRATEGY TO REACH YOUR CANDIDATE POOL**
  - o Identify ways to market the job announcement to reach potential applicants.
  - o Visit or contact the Career Center, Deans, and Professors if you are located on a campus to promote and highlight

the many career opportunities available with ARS.
- o Identify colleagues (both within and outside the organization) who can help in marketing the job.
- o Identify colleges and universities or professional societies and organizations where the announcement should be mailed.
- o Identify newspapers, journals, or online advertising sites that might be useful in marketing the job.
- o Contact the Recruitment Office and your Area Civil Rights Manager for ideas on how to reach a diverse candidate pool.

- *CONTACT YOUR SERVICING HR SPECIALIST*
  - o Discuss recruitment strategies and alternatives, as well as expectations for completion of the action.
  - o Keep in touch with your HR Specialist by e-mail during the recruitment process.
- *SUBMIT ALL REQUIRED PAPERWORK*
  - o Submit all position descriptions and forms needed to request the personnel action.
  - o Submit draft ad text along with the request to save time (remember, your servicing HR Specialist must review and approve all ads prior to being placed).
  - o Submit your "Quality Experience" definition.

WHILE THE VACANCY ANNOUNCEMENT IS OPEN

- ### CONDUCT YOUR MARKETING
  - Be PROACTIVE!
  - Personally identify potential candidates and send a note with the announcement or call to encourage them to apply – **be cautious, however, and don't give the impression they will get the job**.
  - Send the vacancy announcement to individuals, schools and colleges, or organizations you have identified, and place ads in newspapers, magazines, and online job boards.
  - E-mail the announcement to co-workers, colleagues, stakeholders, and peers with a brief note asking for assistance in publicizing the job.
  - Document your efforts.
- ### IDENTIFY A DIVERSE GROUP OF INTERVIEW PANEL MEMBERS AND SET UP PANEL DATES
  - Ask your HR Specialist for an approximate timeframe for receipt of the certificate of eligibles.
  - Ask interview panel members to block out time on their calendars for the interview process.
  - Clear your calendar also!
  - Keep your interview panel members informed throughout the recruitment

process – if conflicts arise, replace panel members immediately.

- ***DEVELOP INTERVIEW QUESTIONS***
  - o Share interview questions with the panel members for comments and suggestions.
- ***CONTACT YOUR HR SPECIALIST THROUGHOUT THE PROCESS***
  - o Ask if you are receiving applications.
  - o Determine if you need to extend the closing date. Ask your HR Specialist to scan applications received to get an idea of the quality of applicants before making a decision to extend the closing date.

ONCE THE CERTIFICATE IS RECEIVED

- ***SCHEDULE THE INTERVIEWS IMMEDIATELY SO THE BEST CANDIDATES ARE STILL AVAILABLE!***
  - o Review the certificate right away and identify the candidates you believe should be interviewed. Ask for help from colleagues as needed. Set a timeframe to complete the interviews.
  - o Schedule the interviews close together to minimize losing a desirable candidate and to maximize the likelihood of remembering individual candidates' strengths and weaknesses.
  - o Have an open mind – interview "Preference Eligible" (Veterans and Displaced) candidates before making judgments on their ability to do the job.

Remember, if they are on the certificate, they meet the qualifications for the position. Talk to your HR Specialist if you have concerns.

- o Advise applicants of your timeframe for conducting the interviews – if they are interested, they will make themselves available.
- o Advise the candidates of the process you will use to conduct interviews (for example, interview panel – give them guidelines).

- **CONDUCT REFERENCE CHECKS**
  - o Always conduct reference checks on top candidates! **This is more critical than ever before.**
- **MAKE YOUR TENTATIVE SELECTION**
  - o Contact the candidate selected to advise that their name is being recommended to Human Resources. Ask if any issues with pay, incentives, EOD, etc.
  - o Notify HR Specialist of your decision and discuss options for offering recruitment incentives. **Remember, the HR Specialist must make the official offer of employment.**
  - o Obtain required area/organization approvals of the selection and incentives being proposed.
  - o Ask the HR Specialist to issue the written employment offer including information on negotiated pay, recruitment incentives and bonuses, and EOD date.

AFTER THE SELECTION IS MADE

- *NOTIFY OTHER CANDIDATES INTERVIEWED OF YOUR DECISION*
  - o HR will notify all non-selected candidates of the final outcome.
  - o Contact the candidates interviewed and encourage them to apply for other positions.
- *SHARE IMPRESSIVE APPLICATIONS*
  - o Share other impressive applications with colleagues who may be recruiting for similar jobs – they can contact and encourage quality applicants to apply for their positions.
  - o Share a copy of other impressive applications with the Recruitment Office – this office can refer the applications to others recruiting for similar positions.
- *PREPARE FOR THE NEW EMPLOYEE'S ARRIVAL*
  - o Make copies of appropriate policies, procedures, and other documents the new employee should read.
  - o Have the employee's workspace cleaned up and the desk stocked with essential supplies.
  - o Prepare the performance plan and provide it along with a copy of the position description on the first day of work.
  - o Set time on your calendar to spend with the new employee on the first day –

show them around the facility, discuss the job and work they will be doing, provide time to read through materials, and let the employee know they can ask questions.

o   Make sure the employee is set up with an e-mail address and computer access, etc.

o   Identify a mentor and develop an Individual Development Plan (IDP) to address with the employee.

o   Inform the employee of the probationary period requirements as well as the promotion potential, if any, of the position.

ASSESSING YOUR RECRUITMENT AND SELECTION PRACTICES

Policies and Procedures

Your organization's policies and procedures should thoroughly document the recruitment, assessment and selection processes. The policies and procedures should be accessible and understood by not only HR professionals but Managers and others involved in the hiring process. Ask yourself these questions to help assess whether or not your organization's policies and procedures are current and include new requirements.

- Are recruitment, assessment and selection processes supported by written policies and procedures that are up-to-date, accurate and complete? *(Ideally within 2 years.)*
- How widely communicated are the organization's written recruitment, assessment and selection policies to those who are involved in the process? *(Ideally to all staff.)*
- Does the organization utilize these policies and procedures for the recruitment, assessment and selection processes?
- Does the organization have a written policy describing procedures for the review of competencies and/or qualifications?
- Does the organization follow a formal recruitment, assessment and selection

125

plan at the start of each recruitment?
(Link to sample recruitment plan)

- Training Managers, supervisors, and personnel involved in the hiring process should receive comprehensive training in the organization's full recruitment process and thoroughly understand proper interview and selection techniques.
- Who performs recruitment activities for the organization? *(Ideally HR with unit management participation.)*
- On average, how long does it take to fill a position within the organization from the start of recruitment until an offer is extended? *(Ideally 2 months or less.)*
- Does the organization provide training and/or written guidelines about recruitment, assessment and selection policies and procedures to managers and supervisors prior to them seeking to fill a position (e.g., reviewing applications, conducting interviews, and evaluating candidates)?

Recruitment Strategies

The organization should tailor their recruitment strategy to meet the need for the specific position and the organization's goals, as well as attract a diverse pool of applicants.

- Does the organization develop a specific recruiting and marketing plan to identify how and who they need to contact to help achieve finding the best candidates?

- Does the organization have a plan to recruit qualified applicants who represent the diversity of the State or local service area?
- Does the organization compare its workforce demographics to the State, county or local labor force demographics?
- Does the organization utilize specialized recruitment strategies to attract hard-to-find, qualified candidates?
- What recruitment strategies are utilized to attract hard-to-find qualified candidates? *(Ideally executive search firms, internet job sites, local and regional newspapers, job fairs, professional organizations, civic organizations, networking, Employment Security Department, etc.)*
- Does the organization track the effectiveness of different recruiting methods?
- Are recruitment sources periodically evaluated to assure they meet the needs of the organization and return on investment calculated?
- Recruitment Process and Hiring
- Recruitment procedures should be developed and administered in compliance with all applicable organization policies, bargaining agreements, laws, regulations, and professional standards.

- Is a job analysis conducted to identify the key responsibilities of a position prior to announcement?
- Are required qualifications reviewed prior to position announcements to assure they are job related?
- Are preferred qualifications reviewed prior to position announcements to assure they are job related?
- Does the organization's HR staff assure all applicants selected for employment meet the posted qualifications for the position?
- What percentage of job announcements identify the competencies needed to perform the job?
- Are essential functions of the position discussed with the candidate?
- Does the organization utilize a behavioral interviewing tool to develop standardized, relevant interview questions?
- Selection Process
- Selection procedures should be developed and administered in compliance with all applicable laws, regulations, and professional standards.
- What methods are used for the selection process? *(Ideally selection matrix, interview notes, resume ranking, skills testing, reference checks, background checks, etc.)*

- What percentage of the final selection decisions is documented? (This includes reasons for hire versus non-hire.)
- How long is the selection documentation retained?
- Does the organization evaluate and assess how well the selection procedures worked?
- How frequently does the organization assess its selection procedures?
- Does the organization maintain documentation of the assessment process?

ADVERTISING, MARKETING, PROMOTIONS, PUBLIC RELATIONS, AND SALES MANAGER JOBS

INDEX*

130

ADVERTISING, MARKETING, PROMOTIONS, PUBLIC RELATIONS, AND SALES MANAGER JOBS

ADVERTISING, MARKETING, PROMOTIONS, PUBLIC RELATIONS, AND SALES MANAGER JOBS